GRAEAE
THEATRE

peeling

by Kaite O'Reilly

peeling was commissioned by Graeae with support from the
Arts Council of England. The script was developed in collaboration
with Graeae through a series of worskhops with Director
Jenny Sealey and Jeni Draper, Lisa Hammond, Caroline Parker
and Sophie Partridge.The first production was assisted by
funding from an Arts Council of England Breakthrough Award.

This is the rehearsal draft, a script still in development. It is likely
to have revisions and changes in performance.

If you require this information in Large Print,
Braille or on Audio Tape please contact
Graeae Theatre Company.

peeling

by Kaite O'Reilly

First performed on 14 February 2002 at The Door, Birmingham Rep, with the following cast:

CAST LIST (alphabetically by character name)

ALFA	Caroline Parker
BEATY	Lisa Hammond
CORAL	Sophie Partridge

CREATIVE & PRODUCTION TEAM

Director & Designer	Jenny Sealey
Lighting Designer	Ian Scott
Costume Designer	Kevin Freeman
Set Realised by	Penny Spedding
Assistant Director	Jamie Beddard
Dramaturg	Phillip Zarrilli
Visual Artist	Mark Haig
Production Manager	Simon Sturgess
Sign Language Advisor	Jean St Clair
	Jeni Draper
Audio Description Advisor	Tim Gebbels
Voice Tutor	Elspeth Morrison
Press	Sally Lycett for Guy Chapman Associates
Marketing	Catrin John
Rehearsal Interpreter	Jeni Draper
Access Officer	Claire Saddleton
Access Worker	Patou Soult

With thanks to:
Paul Sirett, Ben Payne, Sarah Dickinson, Jonathan Meth, Justin O'Shaughnessy at Hoop, Sam Boardman-Jacobs, Annemarie Minkall, the staff of Birmingham Rep and the staff at both the Union Chapel and People Show.

BIOGRAPHIES

ALFA Caroline Parker

Caroline trained at Desmond Jones School of Mime. Theatre credits include *Landscape* (In Tandem Theatre) a one woman show *Walking with Sleepers* (Edinburgh Fringe Festival). Previous Graeae productions include *Two, A Lovely Sunday for Creve Coeur* and *The Changeling*. TV Credits include *Picture This* (Carlton TV). Caroline also has a cabaret act performing well known recorded pop songs (such as Queen's *Bohemian Rhapsody*) in sign language all over the UK.

BEATY Lisa Hammond

Lisa spent three years acting in the popular BBC children's soap *Grange Hill*. Since leaving Grange Hill Lisa has worked on films such as the critically acclaimed *Quills* (Twentieth Century Fox). Recent TV Credits include: *A date with...* (CH4), *Freak out* (CH4), *Focus* (BBC). Recent theatre credits include *Fittings: The Last Freakshow* (Graeae), *Shoot me in the Heart* (Told by an Idiot/The Gate), *King of Fools* (Dash Festival), *A Little Fantasy* (Told by an Idiot/BAC).

CORAL Sophie Partridge

With an Honours Degree in English Major/Art and an arts admin background, Sophie moved to London nearly five years ago. She has since appeared on BBC's *From The Edge*, plus Carlton TV's *Your Shout*. Such brief encounters re-awakened a desire to take up acting. On completion of Graeae's *The Missing Piece* training course, Sophie made her stage debut last February playing Marie in Buchner's *Woyzeck*. After a fleeting TV appearance for *Comic Relief*, in March last year Sophie took her first role with the David Glass Ensemble, as Far Away Alice in the comedy-horror play, *The Unheimlich Spine* and returned to the role recently for its autumn tour.

DIRECTOR/DESIGNER Jenny Sealey

Jenny's professional acting debut was with Graeae Theatre Company. After being a touring actor for eight years she was awarded the Calouste Gulbenkian director training bursary with Interplay Theatre Company. There she co-directed *Sea Changes*, the award-winning *Stepping Stones* and a new opera *Mad Meg*. Jenny returned to Graeae in 1997 as Artistic Director and is fired by the company's policy to explore full artistic accessibility. She has directed all Graeae shows including *Into the Mystic* by Peter Wolf, the critically acclaimed *The Fall of the House of Usher*, the groundbreaking *Fittings: The Last Freakshow*, *A Lovely Sunday for Creve Coeur*, *Alice* (a co-production with Nottingham Playhouse), *Two* and recently *The Changeling*.

Jenny has previously designed *Into the Mystic* and *The Fall of the House of Usher* for Graeae. She lives with her partner Danny Braverman and their son Jonah.

LIGHTING DESIGNER
Ian Scott
Ian is a regular collaborator with Graeae having designed the lighting for *What the Butler Saw*, *Fittings: The Last Freakshow*, *The Fall of the House of Usher*, *Into the Mystic* and, most recently *The Changeling*. Ian trained at Mountview Theatre School. Recent theatre credits: *Casanova* (Suspect Culture), *Unheimlich Spine* (David Glass Ensemble), *Snow Black & Rose Red* (Stratford Circus) and *Passports to the Promised Land* (Nitro).

Other theatre includes: *Caledonia Dreaming* (7:84), *Oh What a Lovely War* and *Frogs* (Royal National Theatre), *Timeless and Mainstream* (Suspect Culture), *Wanted Man* and *Missing Reel* (The Table Show), *Little Violet and the Angel* (Theatre Centre), *The Snow Palace* (Sphinx), *The Beauty Queen of Leenane* (Tron Theatre), *Crazy Horse* (Paines Plough), *The Erpingham Camp* (Assembly, Edinburgh), *Tempest and Monkey in the Stars* (Polka Theatre) and *Invisible Bullets* (Blast Theory).

ASSISTANT DIRECTOR
Jamie Beddard
Jamie Beddard has worked as an actor with Graeae in *Ubu*, *Flesh Fly* and *Alice*, over the last eight years, and is now cutting his teeth as a Director. Outside of the company his TV/film credits include *Skalligrigg*, *Wonderful You* and *Quills*. He is closely involved with Graeae's new writing initiatives, and his first play *Walking Amongst Sleepers* stars Caroline Parker and will be touring later this year.

VISUAL ARTIST Mark Haig
In 1995, Mark discovered the world of video and interactive art through the *Video Positive* exhibition in Liverpool, curated by an electronic arts agency called FACT (The Foundation for Arts and Creative Technology). For the 1997 *Video Positive*, he was asked to create a piece based in Manchester. The result was a film called *24 in 24*, a rendition of 24 hours in post-bomb Manchester time lapsed into 24 minutes. Mark's involvement in multi-media has led to collaborations with Graeae on *Fittings: The Last Freakshow*, *The Fall of the House of Usher* and most recently *Into the Mystic*. Mark has recently worked with The Fittings Group on the stage production of *The Fly* where DVD technology was used to deliver 25 individual scenes which were mixed with a wireless CCTV Camera that provided the 'fly's eye view'.

COSTUME DESIGN
Kevin Freeman

Kevin's previous work includes set and costume design for *The Rose and The Ring*, *Seepage*, *The End of Innocence*, *Sweet Phoebe and Mr Melancholy* (Hen & Chickens), *Desdemona* (Barons Court) and *Wolf Lullaby* (Old Red Lion). Costume design for *Large* (Heart'n Soul, Albany Empire and national tour), and costume construction for *King of Fools* (Dash, Shrewsbury Festival), and recently for Graeae's national tour of *The Changeling*.

SET DESIGN REALISATION
Penny Spedding

Penny has been designing and fabricating props, sculpture, interior designs and bespoke furniture for the last 10 years. Some of her recent commissions include *Nomis* recording studios, *Chitty Chitty Bang Bang*, *Benson & Hedges* promotions, *New Visual Media* (Soho) and *Lloyds* (San Francisco).

WRITER Kaite O'Reilly

Kaite was winner of the Peggy Ramsay Award in 1998 with *Yard,* which was later produced by the Maxim Gorki Theatre, Berlin, as *Slachthaus*. She went on to write and direct *Mouth* for Sgrîn/Channel 4 in 2000. Other productions include *Belonging* at the Birmingham Rep (2000) and *Lives Out of Step* for BBC Radio 3's *The Wire*. Future commissions include Sgript Cymru and Contact, Manchester. Kaite is currently developing her first feature film with an Irish film company.

GRAEAE
THEATRE COMPANY

Established in 1980 by Nabil Shaban and Richard Tomlinson, **Graeae** is Britain's leading theatre company of people with physical and sensory impairments.

Funded by the Arts Council of England, London Arts and London Borough Grants, Graeae tours nationally and internationally twice a year with imaginative and exciting productions of both classic and newly-commissioned theatre.

Graeae's aim is to redress the exclusion of people with physical and sensory impairments from performance and is concerned with developing high quality, genuinely pioneering theatre in both its aesthetic and content.

As well as touring, the company has a strong commitment to training disabled people in performance and other production skills, young peoples' theatre, outreach and education.

Graeae Theatre Company
Hampstead Town Hall, 213 Haverstock Hill, London NW3 4QP

T 020 7681 4755   **F** 020 7681 4756   **M** 020 7681 4757
E info@graeae.org   www.graeae.org

BOARD OF DIRECTORS

Steve Mannix (Acting Chair), Vicky Featherstone, Ben Furner, Dinah Lloyd, Andy Morgan, Ben Payne, Rena Sodhi, Theresa Veith

STAFF TEAM

Artistic Director	Jenny Sealey
Executive Producer	Roger Nelson
Administrator	Annette Cumper
Access Officer	Claire Saddleton
ACE Assistant Director	Jamie Beddard
Finance Consultant	Barbara Simmonds

Kaite O'Reilly
Peeling

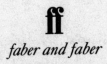

faber and faber

First published in 2002
by Faber and Faber Limited
3 Queen Square, London WC1N 3AU
Published in the United States by Faber and Faber Inc.
an affiliate of Farrar, Straus and Giroux LLC, New York

Typeset by Country Setting, Kingsdown, Kent CT14 8ES
Printed in England by Mackays of Chatham plc, Chatham, Kent

A CIP record for this book
is available from the British Library

ISBN 0–571–21594–7

2 4 6 8 10 9 7 5 3 1

This play is dedicated
to Jenny Sealey

Characters

Alfa, 38
calls herself *an actress*. She is fiercely independent,
eccentric and slightly puritanical. She is Deaf
and uses sign language (both British Sign Language
and Sign-Supported English).

Beaty, 26
calls herself *an actor*. She is fierce, feisty, sexy
and four feet tall.

Coral, 30
calls herself *a performer*. She is small and looks
very fragile, but has a ferocious, inquiring mind.
She uses an electric wheelchair.

Notes

Three women, with outrageous, huge, gorgeous frocks, apparently tied onto large chairs. They are part of the set design for a large production, which is going on unseen elsewhere on stage. The unseen parallel production is an epic visual piece about warfare through the ages – The Trojan Women *updated and with contemporary references. The three women have the occasional moment when they are 'on' as tableaux-fodder and members of the Chorus. Spotlights or floods signify these moments. The rest of the time they are 'unlit', able to relax and chat in the shadows, or comment on the scene before them. However, they are never completely 'off' and they use the devices of the theatre (narration, a form of audio-description, choral speaking, sign interpretation) even when there is no apparent audience. They bicker, play, interrupt – and share the above devices; when one stops, another takes up that role/device. They are constantly shifting and changing, sending each other up, 'ruining' each others' 'moment', taking the piss, passing easily between the formal 'roles' they play – i.e. 'acting' (telling stories, being a narrator/audio-describer etc.) and 'being themselves' (the chat, heckling, etc.). They obviously lie at times: for example in Scene One, when Beaty and Coral pretend not to understand what sign language is, they are using Sign-Supported English (SSE).*

As the play goes on, they change costume, simplifying, stripping down as the parallel unseen production becomes more modern and their stories become more personal and painful. By the end, they are peeled right down to simple underclothes: vests and pants.

One

Darkness.

The stage is suddenly filled with floodlight. Three large mounds are visible – huge dresses, with women sticking out of the top. Two, Coral and Beaty, are in performance mode – poised, highly theatrical – the third dress is empty. As the two women realise there is a vacancy and begin to lose their focus, sudden blackout.

Five seconds pass.

The stage is suddenly filled with floodlight. Three large mounds are visible – all three dresses are inhabited. Alfa, the latecomer, is slightly flustered. The women are static, artificial, poised in a series of tableaux.

As Chorus in a strong post-modern production of The Trojan Women – Then and Now, *they speak/sign to the unseen principles on stage (Hecuba and Andromache), as well as to the audience.*

Chorus

Alfa
Raise your head from the dust.

Beaty
Lift up the throat.

Alfa
Sing.

Coral
Hecuba: This is Troy, but Troy and we are perished.

Beaty
Woman: This is the world, for the verse of destruction you sing is known in other lands.

Alfa
Are we not hurled down the whole length of disaster?

Coral
Throughout history, no change.

Beaty
Troy will be given to the flame to eat.

Coral
Sad birds will sing for our lost young.

Beaty
The city will fall.

Alfa
A horse with its lurking death will come amongst us.

Coral
Children will reach shivering hands to clutch at their mother's dresses.

Beaty
War will stalk from his hiding place.

Coral
We will be enslaved.

Alfa
We will die in our blood.

Beaty
The same, the same, through the long corridor of time.

Beat.

Coral
Gone will be the shining pools where we bathed.

Beaty
Our children will stand, clinging to the gates, crying through their tears.

Beat.

Alfa
 Know nothing. Look for disaster. Lighten your heart.
Go stunned with terror.

 Beat.

Coral
 I lived, never thinking the baby in my womb was born
for butchery . . .

 Long pause.

 *A shift in style. The intensity of lights dips, denoting
 that the women are 'off' and therefore 'themselves':
 professional actors who have been performing the
 Chorus-characters.*

Beaty (*to Alfa*) So where were you? (*to Coral*) I turn
round in the tableau and there's an empty bloody dress
beside me . . .!

Alfa I got stuck, having a fag in the loo. You know how
far backstage it is.

Coral No, I don't, actually. *I* have to cross my legs and
hope for the best. Through the whole epic. All four
hours of it.

Beaty You must have very developed pelvic floor
muscles, then.

Alfa What?

Coral You gave me a right turn, the lights going up and
you not there.

Alfa How d'you think I felt? First time in my life I've
missed a cue. I'm a professional. Things like that don't
happen to me.

Coral They did this time.

Alfa First and only.

Beaty They'll dock your wages.

Alfa So I'll speak to the Equity dep'.

Beaty Director won't like it.

Alfa It won't happen again. I'm sorry, all right? Beaty? Coral? (BSL *only*) SORRY. (*as herself*) It won't bloody happen again.

Beat.

Beaty Every night this play.
Every bloody night this play.
Every night this bloody play.
It gives me a headache.

Pause.
The performers relax slightly, stretch in their cumbersome dresses. Coral takes out a tartan flask and pours out a cup.

Coral Hot chocolate, anyone?

Beaty (AD) < Coral offers us a drink from a tartan flask. > (*as self*) No thanks.

Alfa The wardrobe mistress'll kill you if she catches you eating and drinking in costume. These frocks cost a fortune.

Coral Though quite what significance they have to wars ancient and modern is beyond me.

Beaty Oh, I dunno . . . Every day's a little battle . . . it helps if you face it correctly attired.

Alfa And a bit of luxury can't do any harm. Life's hard enough as it is. I quite like a touch of sumptuous padding.

Coral I feel more like a clothes-horse than a commentator on war.

Beaty It's probably meant to be ironic. (*She takes out a programme and studies it.*) That's what they usually say when they bodge together classic texts with contemporary stuff. Post-modern and ironic.

Alfa (AD) < Beaty refers to a theatre programme for *The Trojan Women – Then and Now* which she handily has under her skirts. >

Beaty (*reading*) Apparently, according to the director's notes, we've all been deconstructed.

Alfa I thought I was being a metaphor.

Coral For what?

Alfa I don't know. I didn't think to ask what the motivation of my metaphor was.

They look at Alfa, then the stage before them. Pause.

Oh, here we go . . .

Coral (AD) < The extras and unseen chorus – >

Alfa (*interjecting, sign only*) THAT IS, US . . .

Coral (AD) < – stare at the stage and the performance going on before them. >

Several beats.

Beaty I hate this bit.

Coral Uummmmm.

Beaty Pretty slow-moving.

Coral Uuummmm.

Alfa 'Interesting' interpretation of Hecuba . . .

Coral Uuummmm.

Several beats.

Beaty Though she is very good.

Alfa Yes, she is, she's very good.

Beaty Marvellous.

Alfa Really.

Coral Uummm.

  Beat.

Beaty Though I could do better.

Alfa Given the chance.

Coral Given the chance . . .

Beaty Given the chance I could definitely do better . . .

  *They sigh, attention begins to wane. Coral puts away
  her flask safely under her skirts.*

Coral They sit.

Beaty They sit.

  Beat.

Alfa My mother'd say this was money for old rope.
  Us sitting here.
  Though she doesn't quite understand how demanding
it is.

  Beat.

Coral It can be taxing.

  Beat.

Alfa To stay in the moment. Focused. Ready for the cue.

Beaty (AD) < We look at her accusingly. Alfa flushes,
recovers, continues. >

Alfa The Chorus to *The Trojan Women* is central.

Beaty Which is why they've left us, shoved at the back,
unlit, onstage.

Beat.

Alfa It's a noble profession.

Beaty I always wanted to go on the stage.

Coral And if we're going to be looked at, anyway, we might as well get paid for it.

Beaty Did your mother tell you that?

Coral No. Did yours?

Beat.

Alfa (*as storyteller*) Once, once . . . Once there was an ancient city . . .

Beaty (*interrupting*) She's off.

Alfa Excuse me . . . ? I'm rehearsing. (*as storyteller*) An ancient city set high –

Beaty (*interrupting*) She does this every night . . . Every bloody night, as if she doesn't know it by heart already . . .

Alfa (*as self*) It's called preparation, you know. And we are here to work. To do a job. For which we get paid. So whilst the principles are warbling on about their fate and the pity of war, I'm going to keep my mind on what I'm supposed to be doing here, thank you very much.

Coral (AD) < Beaty's eyes roll to the heavens. >

Beaty (*mimicking Alfa*) 'I'm a professional, how d'you do? Have a good look, I don't think you've met my kind before.'

Coral (AD) < Despite the half-smiles, a cool, cruel glance passes between them. >

Alfa raises a finger.

Alfa Up yours, lady.

Beaty Ooooh. Will that be in the Sign Language dictionary?

Alfa (*stubbornly*) Once. Once there was an ancient city, high, set high among the olive groves.

Coral (*as self*) And anyway, it's terraces.

Alfa What?

Coral Olive *terraces*. Set high, high among the olive *terraces*.

Alfa That's my line.

Coral Well they'll take it away from you unless you say it right.

Alfa Are you after my lines?

Coral No. I've got my own. But if you can't remember them or get them right . . .

Alfa (*overlapping*) How do you know my part, anyway?

Beaty (AD) < A glint of suspicion enters her eye.>

Coral I've heard it a hundred times!

Alfa No you haven't!

Coral Have!

Alfa Why are you learning my lines?

Coral I'm not!

Alfa You're after my part! You're after . . .

Beaty (AD) < A poison dart of a look whizzes past my ear – an arrow – wwhhhissshhhh – embedding itself firmly into the forehead of Coral, the possible role-stealer . . . The result?

16

All pause, holding breath.

< – sudden silence. >

Alfa Thank you. (*Settles back into storytelling mode.*)
Set high, high among the olive *terraces* and the almond
orchards – an ancient city of women . . .

Beaty It'll have a bad end, wait and see. The ones with
women and children always do.

Alfa Ssh! An ancient city of women and children –
fatherless families – wandering –

Coral sighs hugely, spoiling Alfa's moment.

Beaty (AD) < The most long-suffering sigh slides over
Coral's tongue, rubbing up against her cheeks, then out
over the slightly gappy, could really do with a scrape and
polish horse-like teeth of – >

Alfa (*interrupting firmly*) Fatherless families – wandering
the maze of narrow cobbled streets –

Coral Anyone seen *Eastenders* recently?

Alfa – happy to be together –

Beaty (AD) < A nerve jumps in Alfa's cheek. >

Alfa – grateful that, so far, they have escaped the fate of
Troy . . .

Coral Boorrrriinnnggggg . . .

Beaty (AD) < Coral's eyes roll contemptuously to the
heavens. >

Alfa (*to Coral*) WILL YOU STOP IT!!!!????

Beaty (AD) < Flames blaze in angry eyes – Alfa's mouth
scowls, the lips pucker, > (*as self*) really quite ugly,
actually.

Alfa (*to Beaty*) AND YOU!

Beaty Sorry.

Alfa Christ!

Beaty I was just trying to . . .

Coral takes over Beaty's describing role; the others, in intense conversation, are oblivious to Coral.

Coral (AD) < Her gaze drops, cheeks slightly aflame. >

Alfa Yes?

Beaty I was trying to . . .

Coral (AD) < Beaty's teeth nip on her lower lip, pinching, bloodless . . . >

Alfa What?

Beaty Audio-describe it.

Coral (AD) < She hangs her head, awkward, uncomfortable. >

Alfa Audio –?

Coral DESCRIBE IT, idiot! (*to Beaty*) Bloody hell! She's away with the fairies, you know. Can't keep up. No brain – just mammaries on legs.

Immediately back, as though no interruption.

Audio-describe it.

Alfa And why would you do that?

Beaty Makes it more interesting.

Alfa Only if you can hear.

Beaty and Coral continue, oblivious to Alfa.

Coral I feel quite creative, actually.

Beaty Yeah – I know what you mean.

Coral It's *describing* – innit?

Beaty Yeah.

Coral Like – like painting the scene in visual images that the listener can absorb and internalise and – from spoken words – build that special visual world right inside their own head – in the heart of their imagination.

Alfa Bollix to it, then. It's no bloody good to me.

Beaty Yeah, but then you do all that lovely stuff –

Alfa What?

Beaty Y'know – all that lovely stuff – with your hands.

Alfa (AD) < Beaty and Coral are sign-supporting bits of this as well as speaking. > (*as self*) Sorry?

Coral Oh yeah – I know what you mean – it's lovely.

Beaty Really . . .

Coral . . . Yeah . . .

Both . . . Lovely!

Coral Lovely stuff when you wave them around – your hands – in the air – like . . . like . . .

Beaty . . . like disco-dancing!

Coral Yeah . . .

Beaty (*starts singing and seventies disco-dancing*) D.I.S.C.O.

Coral D.I.S.C. . . .

Alfa (BSL *only*) FUCK OFF! YES . . . TRUE . . . FUCK OFF!

Coral (AD, *simultaneous with the above signing*) < Alfa signs ferociously – >

Beaty (*as self, interrupting*) Viciously –

Coral (AD) < – Beaty and Coral try to translate. >

The following speech is signed in BSL *only, with no voice. Simultaneously, Coral and Beaty try to understand what Alfa is signing.*

Alfa (BSL *only*) . . . FUCK OFF. FUCK RIGHT OFF THE PAIR OF YOU. COWS. MOO. GO AWAY AND MILK YOURSELVES. SQUEEZE YOURSELF DRY OF THAT CYNICISM AND IGNORANCE. PRATS. CHRIST KNOWS HOW I MANAGE, STUCK HERE WITH YOU TWO. I WON'T DO IT AGAIN.

Coral (*translating simultaneously*) Slap hands . . . slap hands together . . .

Beaty (*simultaneous*) Fuck . . . fuck-fucking . . .

Coral Cow . . . noise they make . . .

Beaty/Coral Moo . . . moo . . .

Coral Touch breast . . .

Beaty Tit! Milk cow . . .

Coral Milk ourselves?

Beaty Milk tit fucking . . . cow . . .

Coral Stupid!

Beaty Milk tit fucking stupid cow . . .

Coral Fish! Shape hands make when . . .

Beaty . . . No . . . no no never . . .

Coral . . . Not?

Alfa has finished her signing.

Alfa Amateurs. Bloody amateurs.

Beaty Did you know an avocado stone crushed and combined with yoghurt makes an invigorating and exfoliating shower gel?

Coral Did you know courtesy is catching?

Alfa Did you know we just had our lighting cue?

Floods on. The women pose, high theatricality, then go into Chorus performing mode.

Chorus

Coral
Women of Troy, this is not just your story.

Beaty
Hecuba and Andromache, this infamy has been well read.

Alfa
It has been told and re-enacted, made flesh as the sword marries the bone.

Coral
In that city –

Beaty
In that village –

Alfa
In that settlement, high, up in the hills –

Coral
Low in the valley –

Beaty
Out in the bush –

Alfa
Deep in the city –

Beaty
Women and children –

Coral
Waiting (*beat*) for that feared-for smoke on the horizon.
A smudge at the point where earth meets sky,

Beaty
like a swarm of locusts

Alfa
choking the air

Beaty
beating down between heaven and earth.

Alfa
Fire

Beaty
Smoke

Coral
Pestilence

All (*not without irony*)
Men

Alfa
marching forward with their uniforms

Beaty
and their machetes

Coral
and their orders:

Alfa
To rape

Beaty
To pillage

Coral
To conquer

All
Destroy

Beaty
Slash and burn as they advance, burning the crops,
killing the children –

Alfa
Dismembering limbs –

Beaty
Detaching Achilles' heels so the survivors can't run
away, and so enabling the slaughter to continue,
tomorrow.

Coral
Taking the women for

Alfa
entertainment and pleasure

Beaty
and preferably impregnate them and kill off the line.

Alfa
Woman's body as battlefield.

Beat.

Beaty
Rape as a war tactic.

Beat.

Alfa
Mutilation as a reminder.

Beat.

Coral (*sarcastic*)
Thank God that doesn't happen now.

A brief silence.

Coral

In certain towns they chose to leave the dead where
they fell and kept them so as remembrance – a
memorial of scattered bodies – family members . . .
neighbours . . . the schoolmaster . . . midwife . . .

*Beat. Beaty says the following as a Chorus member
telling a personal testimony.*

Beaty

I had gone away that day, walking through the bush
to the medical centre. I went alone. My little brother
cried to join me, but I was a grown girl, on serious
business. What use would he be to me? I made him
stay home. When I returned, our soldiers stopped me
from going to my village. They said there had been
a massacre. A rival tribe. There was one survivor.
People were hanging from the trees. Others lay in a
pile of bodies in the schoolhouse, where they had
been taken to be slaughtered. My brother was in the
schoolhouse. He was curled, on his knees, covered by
the body of my mother, who had tried to save him.
They had been butchered.
The survivor was me.

Alfa (AD) < The lights go down. Ladies and gentlemen:
a brief interlude. >

*Pause. The lights go off. The women are 'off', now
'themselves'.*

Coral I don't think I like this play very much.

Beaty (AD) < She shivers. Somewhere, big boots are
walking over her grave. >

Coral Don't.

Alfa (AD) < Alfa disappears from out of her dress. >

Alfa unstraps herself and disappears behind her dress.

24

Beaty What's made you squeamish all of a sudden?

Coral Nothing, nothing, I . . . what!? Do you think something's different?

Beaty No.

Coral Good, because there isn't. I'm just . . .

Beaty (AD) < She shrugs, grimaces, runs a hand over her lined face. >

Coral You know how sometimes when a show opens and it's been running a while and you get used to it and you go onto auto-pilot a bit . . .?

Pronounced pause.

(AD) < Beaty bites her lips, puffs her cheeks out a little, is reluctant to admit she knows what I'm talking about. >

Beaty . . . Maybe . . .

Coral I know you're not supposed to go on auto-pilot, but . . . I've just crash-landed.

Beaty (AD) < Coral struggles, pulls a face. >

Coral . . . I . . .

Beaty (AD) < Her eyes hook into mine, urgent with meaning, but unfortunately I haven't got a bloody clue what she's talking about. > (*as self*) What?

Coral I'm feeling it more. I've done it a hundred times, the mouth moving, words coming out, but I . . . I'm feeling it more . . . and . . . I don't like it.

Beaty Just don't let it get to you.

Coral But some of the stories, the modern ones, they're . . .

Beaty (*interrupting*) You think too much. *Feel* everything too much. Travel light. Go naked. Chill.

Coral Doesn't it get to you?

Beaty No. 'Cause as an actress, I'm a carnivore – I like strong meat. So the stories are full-on . . . Would you rather be in music theatre?

Coral No!

Beaty Well then . . .

Coral . . . but . . .

Beaty What!?

Coral Well, I don't know . . . just sometimes . . . I'd like to do something . . . upbeat –

Beaty Fantasy?

Coral No – positive. Uplifting. With a happy ending.

Beaty Yeah. Fantasy.

Alfa Who'd like some soup?

Beaty (AD) < Alfa appears from behind her dress, with some carrots, a bowl, and her blender. >

In the following section, the women may unstrap themselves from their dresses and move around. Alfa will probably be very active in the making of her soup.

Alfa I never go anywhere without this. (*She revs up her blender.*) Hand-held, runs on batteries, hugely versatile . . . a life-saver.

Beaty (AD) < She begins making soup. >

Alfa does.

Alfa Well, while there's a lull in the action, we might as well make the most of it. And that useless stage manager isn't going to bring us any refreshments. He's terrified of me. I'm sure he thinks 'deafness' is catching.

Beaty It is, if you're close to his ear and you shout loud enough.

Alfa (AD) < Alfa busies herself with grating carrots. As she is refusing to make eye contact, and is the main signer, that closes down that source of communication for a while – Beaty and Coral know this. >

Coral (AD) < Coral squirms on her chair, takes out a half-deflated kiddies' rubber swimming ring with a duck's head and starts to blow it up. >

Beaty (AD) < Beaty takes out some risqué lingerie, sequins and a needle and thread. Coral notices Beaty's g-string – >

Coral (AD) < – largely because she's waving it around (some would say showing it off) generously displaying its crotchless nature . . . >

Beaty What can I say? Life's short: enjoy . . .

Coral Moonlighting, are we? I've heard you can earn, oooh, five quid an hour in some of the booths in Soho, if you're lucky.

Beaty Piss off, you're only jealous.

Smiling with anticipation, Beaty busies herself with choosing and sewing a sequin onto her evening attire.

Coral What's the occasion?

Beaty I've a new boyfriend.

Coral Is he lush?

Beaty Gorg'. You can see him yourself. He's picking me up at the end of the show and I do so like customising what I wear to bed.

Coral (AD) < She continues with her adult-rated needlework. Coral inflates the ring, then settles it under

her skirts. She wobbles onto it, sighs with contentment, >
(*as self*) I'm a martyr to haemorrhoids. (AD) < She sits
with great contentment, looking about her, watching her
industrious colleagues. > (*as self*) Make do and mend.
(*new thought*) Preferably with cat gut. My body is criss-
crossed with scars like a railway track. Like Crewe
Station, seen from the air: single tracks, with no
apparent destination; major interlocking junctions,
where intercity, sleepers and local lines all connect.
Puckering scar tissue, hand-sewn with careless, clumsy
stitches. I like to finger it, trace the journeys. That
unborn skin: smooth, intimate – the coral-pink colour
of mice feet. It's beautiful. I love it. Given the choice,
I'd never have it any other way, now.

Pause.

Are you listening, Mother?

Pause.

Do you hear me, Mother?

*Several beats. Alfa, still preparing her soup, uses her
blender as punctuation during the following:*

Alfa Mine used to warn me about men. (*as her mother*)
'You keep your hand on your ha'penny. You'll have to if
you want any kind of chance with a man. It's bad enough
you being damaged goods. He'll not want you if you're
second-hand, thumbed through and used already.'

Coral Ouch!

Alfa I didn't pay any attention, though. You wouldn't,
either, if you saw the cardigans she wore. . . . But
bless . . . I love my mum . . .

Coral (AD) < Beaty and Coral exchange a look of . . . >

Beaty/Coral (AD) < Envy. >

Beaty (*as her mother*) 'You have to entice; you have to beguile. Put it all in the shop window, Beatrice, though God knows you have little enough. Put yourself on special offer, girl.'

Coral Mothers . . . who'd be one, eh?

Beaty They love to maim.

Alfa But they think it's for our own good. Tough love. They're trying to help.

Beaty Absolutely. Because we don't want to get too big for our boots, do we?

Coral And we mustn't aspire to other things . . . We have to be kept in our places.

Beaty (*as her mother*) 'Keep your aim low and you'll never be disappointed . . . You have a short shelf-life, Beatrice.'

Coral She's got a way with words, your mother.

Beaty When they buried her, I had the greatest temptation to laugh down into that hole they were putting her in: 'So who was it survived the longest, then?' She was convinced she'd see me out.

Coral Was it sudden, then?

Beaty For her, yes. Had no idea she was going. But I knew. To the tick. It's a talent I have – I've been thoroughly trained in it – to sense time passing and my old mate, the grim reaper, stalking close behind. All my life, thanks to my mum, I've felt the tip of his scythe touching the nape of my neck. My mother was so focused on that, waiting for me to croak, she didn't notice the big fingers come to snuff her out. So I buried her. There's not many with 'reduced life-expectancy' can say that. It's an achievement. There's not many like me can press the earth down on their mother's face. Stamp on the grave. Put a layer of concrete over so she can't rise again. I joke of course.

Coral Of course.

Beaty Though she was the joker in our family. She'd call me into the bathroom and make me stare at her face. She was getting deep crow's feet around her eyes – she hated it – and the skin around her jaw line was beginning to soften – sag a bit – her face covered in fine hairs, like the fur of a peach. And she'd cradle her face in her hands and stretch back the skin so the wrinkles would disappear and she'd say, 'That's what I looked like when I was sixteen. You're lucky, Beatrice. Just think, you'll never have lines on your face like me – you'll never see your features blurring, you'll never suffer from the ravages of age. You're so lucky, Beatrice. You're so lucky you'll die when you're young. You're so lucky you'll never live to be old.'

Several beats.

Alfa Has anyone got any Neurofen?

Coral Are you starting?

Alfa I'm in the most terrible pain.

Beaty You look pretty crap.

Alfa That's the pain.

Coral You want to eat bananas when you're on your period.

Beaty You do look crap.

Alfa I can't help it.

Beaty Ever heard of make-up?

Coral They're rich in potassium, which is exactly what you need.

Alfa I look crap even when I wear make-up.

Coral Or Evening Primrose Oil, that's good.

Beaty You look crap.

Alfa I look so crap because I'm in such pain.

Coral And Star Fruit. That's the new one.

Alfa I have to have an operation.

Coral Yeah, well, I'm on my period.

Alfa And the pills I have to take . . .

Beaty I shit pills. They shoot out like coins from a slot machine in Vegas. Just chug chug chug, all nudges and triples. It's the amount of tablets I have to take. For my pain. When I walk down the road I rattle.

Alfa You rattle? I'm like a broken washing machine. On spin.

Coral Yeah, but at least you don't have your period.

Alfa I am a wreck. In emotional and physical pain. I am embodied pain. I am the physical embodiment of emotional and physical pain.

Coral I get body cramps. Even my hair hurts when I'm having my period.

Beaty I lose my vision.

Alfa I lose my hearing and I'm deaf.

Coral I'm on the toilet so much I might as well have it moved into the lounge so I can sit on it and watch the telly.

Alfa Why don't you just go around with a bucket between your legs?

Beaty I can't have children.

Coral I'm pregnant.

Alfa What's that about being on your period, then?

Coral I was being nostalgic.

Beaty and Alfa laugh. Coral doesn't. Beaty notices the lighting cue.

Beaty There's the lights – they're changing.

Alfa I know it's only a brief interlude, but it gets briefer every night. I haven't had my soup, yet.

Coral (AD) < We swiftly put away our toys as Alfa climbs into her dress. >

Alfa I swear it's just so the crew can make last orders at the bar.

Beaty Well, you have to get your priorities right . . .

The women take a moment to prepare for the next scene – some breathing, focus work, done seriously.
  Floods come on. The women move into stylised tableaux, establishing the change in dynamic for the 'parallel' play. Alfa continues as storyteller, the story she was rehearsing earlier. The others follow, as Chorus.

Chorus

Alfa
  Once, once there was an ancient city, high, set high among the olive terraces and the almond orchards – an ancient city of women and children, fatherless families – wandering the maze of narrow cobbled streets – happy to be together – grateful that, so far, they had escaped the fate of Troy.

Coral
  These women had lost their men to some fruitless battle over some unknown argument rooted centuries before . . .

Beaty
These women knew in which direction the world
revolved and it was counter to them.

Alfa
They smelt the ash of a thousand burning bodies and
sensed the military advance, watching the bruise of
smoke deepen on the delicate flesh where the earth
and the sky met.

Coral
And these women knew the stories:

Beaty
Rape as a war tactic. Babies' heads split like conkers.

Coral
And they knew what would happen . . .

Beat.

Alfa
So they made a decision, those women with their
children in the ancient city high in the hills, amongst
the flowering almond blossom and the olive terraces:
They taught their children to dance –

Beaty
Mamma's precious

Coral
Future joy

Alfa
– they taught their children to dance and, clasping
hands, they danced up along the city gates

Beaty
as the bruise deepened on the horizon,

Alfa
they danced out, along the city's upper walls, past the
lookout –

Coral

where the armour of the approaching army was
clearly visible, glinting in the light.

Alfa

Beyond the cobbled roads, where the path stumbled
into rock and mud they danced, up along the steep
incline, hands clasped, tiny feet stamping the rhythm –

Beaty

Mamma's precious

Coral

Future joy

Alfa

– up towards the pinnacle,

Beaty

as the soldiers grew closer,

Alfa

where tiny feet faltered but were urged on, hands
clasped, dancing, dragged –

Coral

Mothers' faces wet with tears –

Alfa

feet dancing, on and on until there was no more land
to dance on and their feet tripped on air and, hands
clasped, dancing, dancing, they danced out and
plummeted to their deaths.

*Beat, floods off, the women still in chorus mode, but
no longer 'on'.*

Beaty (AD) < There is a pause in Alfa's signing hands – a
hesitation before her fingers – the children and Mothers –
descend. Descend. >

Coral (AD) < Beaty's eyes fill with tears. >

Beaty No they don't.

Alfa (AD) < She stares at Coral viciously. >

Beaty They don't.

Coral Okay.

Beaty Say it.

Coral (AD) < Beaty's eyes do not fill with tears. >

Beat.

Beaty (*as self*) Thank you. (*as storyteller*) Some versions claim that heavenly creatures swooped and caught the fragile bodies before they smashed into the rocks below. Spared pain, delivered to safety, a happy ending, stopping our minds from imagining the broken, mangled bodies – bones splintering on impact, children's screams as they realise Mamma isn't to be trusted, after all –

Coral Versions that save us from the horrific contemplation of the mothers' decisions and those last terrible moments . . .

Coral can't say it. Finally Beaty does for her.

Beaty . . . Killing your own child.

Alfa As you've probably gathered, this is not one of those versions.

Beaty But we don't believe in the pretty stories, the 'being spared all that' – the lies. We believe in knowing the full picture so you can prepare yourself for the worst –

Coral – but also – why not? – hope for the future . . .?

Alfa Finished?

Beaty Yes. Thanks.

Coral I told you I'd already heard it.

Blackout.

Two

Alfa is knitting, Beaty reading an up-market gossip magazine and Coral making changes with her costume. Beaty's magazine-related lines should be up-to-date, show-biz gossip taken from the week of performance. Stars' names (*) should be changed to the latest flavour of the month.

Alfa I sometimes think my entire life is spent behind screens: at the hospital, here at the theatre, and when I'm sign-interpreting, I'm always kept apart, away from the action.

Coral In a performance, when it's happening, do you –

Beaty (*cutting Coral off*) I think there's something really sinister about Chris Evans* and Billie Piper.*

Coral What?!

Alfa Even at the hospital I've a bit part. (*as Nurse*) 'Pop your clothes off and the doctor will be with you in a moment' – all the drama and interesting shenanigans happen the other side of the screen to me.

Beaty (*of magazine*) I like her hair colour. D'you think it'd suit me?

Coral What?!

Alfa But it's even worse here – I'm an *actor* – I should be full of *action* rather than the passive recounter of doom.

Beaty (*of magazine*) Jesus, she's really put on weight.

Coral Beaty, d'you mind putting down the magazine and giving me a hand with the costume-change?

Beaty I'm busy.

Coral Please?

Alfa The done-to, that's me.

Coral Pretty please?

Alfa I'm never the doer.

Coral Alfa?

Beaty She's busy knitting.

Coral Well, piss off, the lot of you, then.

Beaty Ooooh . . . Madam . . .

Alfa Is she getting a strop on?

Beaty Yeah.

Alfa She does that.

Beaty Yes, she does do that –

Alfa Get a strop on –

Beaty I know.

Alfa Terrible.

Beaty Not enough sex –

Alfa – or chocolate –

Beaty – or both –

Alfa/Beaty – at the same time.

Alfa Oh – she didn't like that.

Beaty No – she didn't like that.

Alfa (AD) < Alfa admires Coral's disapproving little pout. >

Coral I haven't got a disapproving little pout.

Alfa (AD) < Coral's pinching facial expression tells otherwise. >

Coral That's not fair. You're describing me all wrong.

Beaty (AD) < Her face shrivels with indignation, becoming mean, ugly and malignant like a tumour. >

Coral Oh great, insult by audio-description.

Beaty (AD) < Her lips pucker; her nostrils flare self-righteously. >

Coral They did not do that! I couldn't do that if I tried!

Alfa (AD) < Coral tries to be the indignant ingenue, but is unfortunately too old to play that part. >

Coral You're not telling the truth!

Alfa You're in a war play, dearie. Surely you know in a war play, the first casualty is truth?

   Pause.

Remember that time we were appearing in *Metamorphosis* in Watford and there was a fire? (*as Deputy Stage Manager*) 'Mr Sun is in the building . . .' and they evacuated the theatre, but left us beetled-up on stage? She got stroppy then, as well.

Coral I wasn't a dung beetle. I was playing a black widow spider, stuck upside down in some kind of web.

Beaty Yeah, I remember – that giant rope ladder from the Army and Navy Stores.

Alfa None of it adequately fire-proofed. We could have fried.

Coral Us and the wheelies abandoned in the front row. Just as well it was a false alarm.

Alfa And after, when they realised they'd left us, that bloody theatre manager running round screaming:

Coral (*hijacking story*) 'And this is why "*handicaps*" are a health and safety risk.'

Beaty Prick.

Alfa There was cause, *then*, to be judgemental, to get a strop on. That was justified.

Beaty (*flicking through her magazine*) Now, Michael Douglas* . . . I wouldn't touch him with a bloody bargepole.

Alfa I wouldn't touch anyone. I'm more a unicycle than a tandem these days, if you get my meaning. Unless you want a family, or you've met the love of your life – which I think is a myth – why bother? Life's complicated enough as it is.
 Did you know that women over thirty in New York are more likely to develop cancer *and* be a victim of violent crime than have a lasting monogamous relationship with a straight man?

Beaty Did you know when you mix avocado and garlic and lemon juice, you get guacamole?

Alfa Did you know the end of the world is nigh?

Coral Did you know the most famous disabled woman is Helen bloody Keller?

Beaty Is that her name? Helen Bloody-Keller? As in double-barrelled?

Coral But to people she's the Marvellous Helen Bloody-Keller, a sort of super-spas'.

Alfa 'Disabled people are the heroes of our time.' Peter Brook said that.

Coral Heroes for whom?

Alfa Exactly.

Beaty Peter Brook as in *The Man Who Mistook His Wife for a Hat*?

Coral No. Peter Brook as in 'the director who mistook exploitation for disability politics'.

Beaty (AD) < Beaty checks her watch, then reluctantly puts away her magazine. > (*as self*) Get out the canary, we're back to the coal-face . . .

Coral We're not on for a while, yet.

Beaty So where are we, then?

Coral Towards the end of Act Two: The fall of Troy and slaughter of the innocents.

Alfa Oh, I like that bit . . . (AD) < The extras – i.e. us – stare, with varying levels of involvement, at the dramatic scene going on before them. >

They do so.

Coral (*as self*) In a performance, when it's happening, do you . . .

Beaty/Alfa . . . Sssssh.

Coral (AD) < Beaty and Alfa are enthralled, lip-syncing the actors, upstaging them in the dark – > (*as self*) – like they do in this scene, every bloody night.

Beaty I'd love to play Andromache. I could do it better than *her*.

She refers to the (unseen) performer on stage.

(*As Andromache*)
I nursed for nothing. In vain the labour pains and long sickness –

Alfa Oh, bless.

Beaty (*as Andromache*)
I have no strength to save my children from execution
Nor the children of other mothers –

Alfa/Beaty
– who are suffering no less than me.

Coral (*as self*) In a performance, when it's happening,
do you –

Alfa/Beaty Ssssh . . .

Beaty (*as self*) I love this bit . . .

Coral (AD) < In synchronicity, they shift, heads moving,
following the action about the stage. >

> *They do so for some time, Alfa and Beaty creating the*
> *illusion of watching an emotional scene in the unseen*
> *parallel play. This continues under the following text.*

Alfa (*as self*) They're going to kill her little boy . . .
(BSL *only*) BEAUTIFUL.

> *Alfa makes another happy, heartfelt sigh, reacting to*
> *what's happening 'onstage'.*

Coral (AD) < Coral's attention wanders. >

Alfa So poignant . . . I wish someone would let me do a
scene like that.

Alfa/Beaty Oh!

Alfa (*as Andromache*)
Child, your fingers clutch my dress.
What use, to nestle like a young bird under the
mother's wings?

(*quietly, as self*) Fantastic . . .

Alfa/Beaty (*as Andromache*)
I cannot help you.

Alfa (*as Andromache*)

My voice is hoarse from shouting, but no one hears . . .

(*As self*) They're stuffed. No power, no hope, just the boys marching in and –

Beaty (*as self*) I can't look at this bit when they take the baby. Have they taken him yet? Have they taken her baby?

Alfa (*as self*) Well, that's fate, when you're Hector's child . . . You've got to be sacrificed . . . They can't keep alive a dead hero's son . . .

Beaty Bastards.

Alfa They're just following orders.

Beaty Killing off the line . . .

Coral (AD) < Coral's attention continues to wander, further out into the auditorium. >(*as self*) In a performance, when it's happening, do you –

Alfa/Beaty – Ssssh . . .

Coral (AD) < They are engrossed. Eyes on stalks. >

Alfa They'll never see each other again . . .

Beaty I can't . . . (look)

Coral (AD) < Their attention is pinned to the action like an Amazonian butterfly onto a dusty baize presentation board. >

Alfa (*whispered, to unseen players*) Just . . . Yes . . . Hold . . . hold . . .

Coral (AD) < Alfa, unseen, conducts the actors onstage. >

Alfa That's it . . . yeees . . . hooollld . . . hooolllldd . . .

Beaty Two . . . three . . .

Alfa And releeeaaassse . . .

Alfa/Beaty There!

Coral (AD) < Alfa and Beaty smile satisfied and strangely self-congratulatory at each other. >

Alfa That timing!

Beaty That was really good.

Alfa Her discipline!

Beaty Well, eight years doing psychophysical work . . .

Alfa Exactly! I mean . . .

Coral (AD) < They nod. Reminiscent of those little toy dogs that were put in the back windows of cars in the seventies. >

They nod.

(*As self*) But not our car, because we couldn't afford a car.

Alfa I love seeing good work. Makes it all worthwhile.

Beaty They did that scene really well . . .

The magic of performance wears off, returning Beaty to her brittle self.

Let's hope the rest of the show doesn't suffer because of it . . .

Coral (AD) < Coral looks at the action, then out towards the audience. > (*as self*) In a performance, when it's happening, do you ever watch the audience watching the show?

Alfa No.

Coral You just sit there and ignore what's going on in front of you!?

Alfa Yes. D'you want a hand with your costume change?

Coral Please.

Beaty (AD) < The performers help each other out of their big flashy dresses, revealing yet another frock underneath. >

> *The performers help each other out of their big*
> *dresses, revealing another underneath.*
> *Alfa makes an audio description of the actual*
> *costumes used in performance, then:*

Coral Is this a posh war, or what? Red silk dresses . . .

Alfa Don't knock it. I'm hoping to keep mine, afterwards.

Coral It doesn't feel right.

Alfa What do you want? A horsehair shirt?

Coral I thought we'd be in khaki.

Alfa We're the Chorus of a war play, not Kate bloody Adie. And the costume designer did train with Jean-Paul Gaultier . . .

Beaty We could have ended up with conical tits! Imagine: us lifted, separated and strategically aimed . . .

Alfa I'd rather that than some worthy interpretation. The Furies or Fates. Or the bloody Graeae sisters, with an eye and tooth shared between them . . .

Coral And, God forbid, if we were them, we might be meaningful and have to be taken seriously – given some status instead of bit parts, in the shadows. You know, it's a shame your wonderful costume designer didn't just build us into the scenery, so they could have done away with our bodies and contribution altogether.

> *Beat.*

Beaty What's bitten you?

44

Alfa Oh, don't complain to anyone about the dresses . . . please don't take away my one little luxury . . . life's hard, please, please don't put us in khaki . . .

Coral You're right, I see that now. If we were dressed in khaki, that might suggest reality and make the audience think about *us* and what we're *saying* rather than the quality and texture of what we're wearing on our backs . . . Don't look at me like that. (AD) < Pensive, calculating – their mouths shrewish, eyes narrowed. > (*as self*) It wasn't *me* acting along with the principles, ready to sell *my* soul for a decent part . . . It wasn't *me* lip-syncing Andromache . . .

> *Beat.*

Don't you get tired of being the decoration . . . the mute mime show . . . the right-on extras stuck at the back whilst the *real* actors continue with the *real* play . . .?

Alfa I'm tired of sign-interpreting a performance but never getting the chance to perform it *properly*.

Coral Well, I've had it with bath chairs. I'm not doing a period piece again. And my agent . . . if he ever puts me up again for a casting for *Aliens* . . .

Alfa (*emphatically interrupting*) Don't. Go. There.

Beaty (AD) < Beaty has been watching all this silently, her teeth lightly catching on the ulcer growing on the inside of her mouth. > (*as self*) Well, if I get a job, it's down completely to my talent.

Coral Yeah, the talent to be the ticked box on an equal-opportunities monitoring form.

Beaty My, aren't we bitter and twisted?

Coral No, even when we're ideal for the part, we don't get it.

Beaty Look, I know you would have been a brilliant Hedda Gabler and you were born to play Joan of Arc, but disappointments happen and you just have to –

Coral (*interrupting*) You know what I mean.

Beaty . . . No. Don't use excuses and don't include me in your *résumé* of failure.

Coral Excuses!

The following dialogue overlaps: all speak/sign quickly and simultaneously – creating a moment of chaos and poor communication.

Beaty It's a tough business.

Coral Even when it's a disabled character, they give it to a walkie-talkie.

Beaty No one said it would be easy.

Alfa Cripping up. The twenty-first century's answer to blacking up.

Beaty If you can't run with the big dogs, stay on the bloody porch.

Coral My agent was telling me there's talk of doing a bio-pic about Tamara Detreaux –

Overlap ends as though it never happened.

Alfa Tamara . . .?

Coral A bio-pic about Tamara Detreaux. You know, the Hollywood actress who played E.T. . . .?

Beaty Really?

Coral Yeah.

Beaty They're casting?

Coral Apparently.

Beaty When!? I'd be perfect! I'd be absolutely perfect for . . .

Coral They're gonna cast either Angelina Jolie* or Penelope Cruz*, then digitally shrink her down to size.

Beaty You Are Joking.

Coral Nope. Computer generation. It's the future.

Alfa So then – d'you think they could film you two, then blow you up to size?

Beaty I am 'to size', thank you, fuck-face.

Alfa You have such a problem with aggression.

Beaty No – I have such a problem with you being a fuck-wit.

Alfa And your language! I really don't like it. I don't like signing all those fucks, you know.

Coral (AD) < Alfa signs 'fuck' repeatedly and with violence. It is not a pretty sight. >

Alfa (*signs and speaks*) Fuckfuckfuckfuckfuckfuckfuck-fuckfuck

Pause.

Coral Do you think we all end up just like our mothers? If we had kids, would we make the same mistakes?

Alfa Where did that come from?

Coral Nowhere . . . just . . . (*to Beaty*) In a performance, when it's happening, do you ever watch the audience watching the show?

Beaty Yes. I make a mental note of who yawned and who forgot to switch off their mobile phone, then I have a contract taken out on them.

Alfa The magic of theatre. Live performance as a collaborative act, the dynamic created by the relationship between the spectacle and the spectators. That's why no two performances are the same. It's symbiotic.

Beaty Exactly. And if the audience don't respect that, they're asking for their legs to be broken . . . (AD) < We look out at the audience expectantly. >

Several beats as they stare at the audience expectantly.

(AD) < Slowly the expectation turns to boredom and disappointment. Only Coral remains staring. >

Coral I watch them – the audience – their heads sleek in the dark – furtive – secretive, with their little habits, tics, inappropriate coughs, gaze. I watch them – but it's transgressive – I'm to be stared at, not them. But I look and I want to ask, who are you? Why are you here? What do you think of me? As you sit there in your rows in the dark rubbing shoulders with strangers, looking, listening – what do you think of me? Am I just another performer? What am I? My mother could never find the *exact* word for me – even though she's still searching. (*as her mother*) 'What are you like, Coral? I'll tell you what you're like: a disappointment. A let-down. And after all my sacrifices . . .' (*to audience as self*) I'm watching you.

Beat.

Beaty We're on.

The performers possibly go into a series of tableaux denoting battle and warfare. If so, each image should be audio-described.

Chorus

Coral
And as the battle commenced and the

Beaty
heat-seeking missiles

Alfa
  arrows

Beaty
  bayonets

Coral
  stones found their mark and as the

Alfa
  soldiers

Coral
  mercenaries

Beaty
  widow-makers

Coral
  serial killers

Alfa
  former-neighbours advanced

All
  on both sides;

Coral
  and as the mortar

Alfa
  shrapnel

Beaty
  boiling oil

Coral
  poured down,

Alfa
  we sat in the ruins and laughed:

All
  Haven't we been here, before?

Coral

And as the radio blared

Alfa

and the spider shuttled back and forth into the corner

Beaty

and the children were taught marching songs in the courtyard

Alfa

we signed their death warrants

Coral

by not saying

All

no.

Alfa

Child – I should have taken your nursery pillow and suffocated you myself rather than leave you to bleed dry on no-man's-land.

Beaty

I should have crushed you in the womb – folded you back inside myself rather than let you die by suicide bomb in a crowded discotheque.

Coral

Her hope is that he died, dancing –

Beaty

Mamma's precious

Alfa

Future joy

Beaty

hands clasped, dancing, dancing . . .

Alfa signs a version of the 'dance of death' as at the end of Scene One.

Coral (AD) < Alfa's fingers dance, dancing, dance down the deaths . . . >

> *Beat.*
>> *The moment is slowed, completed. Floods go off.*
>> *A beat.*

Coral I'm pregnant.

> *Beat.*

Alfa (*to Beaty*) She's pregnant.

Beaty How?

Coral Immaculate conception second time round. How d'you think?

Alfa She shagged somebody. A man. Shagged him.

Coral And this is doing my head in . . . This play is . . . help me.

Beaty What?

Coral Help me by telling me . . .

Beaty What d'you want me to say?

Coral That it'll be all right. That . . . that earth's an okay place to take a baby . . . That . . . I'd be a good mum . . . That . . .

Beaty But we don't know that, do we?

Coral What?

Beaty Any of it. We don't know any of it.

Coral But tell me.

Beaty I can't answer that. I don't know.

Coral Please . . .

Beaty You want me to lie?

> *Beat.*

Alfa (AD) < Coral looks at Beaty, who doesn't speak. Alfa takes out her knitting. >

Beaty (AD) < Beaty sets up her mirror, takes out her wig and prepares for the next scene. >

They do as described.

Coral Please.

Alfa (AD) < A painful pause. >

A painful pause.

(*as self*) How about the dad?

Coral Gone. Not worth it anyway. Better off without him.

Beaty Why'd you get pregnant if you didn't want to get pregnant?

Coral It wasn't planned.

Alfa Were you taken by force?

Coral No . . . It seemed a good idea at the time.

Beaty I've a really nice recipe for sweet potatoes. You put them in olive oil and in the oven, and when they come out, they're all really nice and soft.

Alfa Is there a low-fat version?

Coral It'd be irresponsible for me to have a baby I don't really want.

Beaty Exactly. Story over. Move on.

Alfa Sod it, I've dropped a stitch.

Coral (*to Beaty*) Are things always so black and white to you?

Beaty Yeah.

Alfa (*to Beaty*) You know – that wig really suits your skin colour.

Coral But it doesn't stop me from thinking about it. It's real. It could happen. I could have . . . I could . . . If things were different, I'd have it. I'd like to look after it in a family – what's that stupid word? Nuclear? Nuclear family. Only I'd have mum, dad, baby and fucking personal assistant. I wouldn't do that, subjecting a baby to that. No privacy. Every Tom Dick or Harriet sticking their noses in and the mood of the day dependent on some mardy PA: 'Why, you've really fucked me up and over today, how very *caring* of you . . .' A baby couldn't grow up in that. All those people . . . passed around, one pair of stranger's hands to another. Not knowing whose arms are holding you. Watching mummy be patronised, treated as an incompetent; some kind of Frankenstein with her new-born baby. I couldn't put a child through that. I couldn't. Never mind everything else – how unsafe the world is . . . how suddenly filled with sharp edges and . . .

Beaty (*rudely interrupting*) Great. Decision made. End of conversation.

Coral No! I was still speaking, I was . . .

Beaty Shit, or get off the pot.

Coral What?!

Beaty You're going on and on and on. Make the decision. Or if you're going to whinge, be a bit more entertaining, would you?

Coral What's wrong with you?

Beaty You wittering on about this frigging baby.

Alfa It's not a baby. It's a collection of cells. A blood clot. Little more than a minor thrombosis and nothing you say will convince me otherwise.

Beat.

Coral Well, thank you, both. This is probably the most important decision I'll ever make in my life. I thought you'd understand, help me think it through, but no. Who was I kidding? Just forget it. Just forget I ever said anything.

Beaty Ooooh. Little Miss Tantrum . . .

Coral Conversation closed.

Beaty Don't take it out on us that the one time you shag in your life you get caught.

Coral Dialogue finito.

Beaty Wasn't us that put you up the duff, off the rag and in the family way.

Coral Just leave it.

Beaty Why?

Coral Just . . .

Beaty Why?

Coral Because you wouldn't know a helpful, sympathetic thing to say if it jumped up and bit you in the arse. Because you don't understand.

Beaty (*interjecting*) No?

Coral Because you're so lacking in the milk of human kindness, you've gone rancid. Because you haven't the slightest idea . . .

Beaty (*interrupting*) I've had to make the same decision.

Beat.

I've had a child. But I've not been a mother. I've had a child. But it's not the same.

Coral Isn't it?

54

Beaty It doesn't count. I had all the biology . . . the physical sensations – that new life moving under my hand –

Alfa (*in sign only*) FISH UNDER ICE.

Beaty – stirring inside –

Alfa (*in sign only*) NIGHT SWIMMING.

Beaty – waking me in the night . . .

Coral But you haven't mothered?

Beaty No.

Alfa And it's not the same.

Beaty (*to Alfa*) And you'd know about that, would you?

Alfa I know a sad woman when I see one.

Beaty Know all about babies? About carrying them and giving birth?

Alfa Ugly and sad. It's there, in your mouth.

Coral (AD) < Alfa's hand shapes the air. >

Alfa I can see it. (AD) < Sorrow. The lips pulling down, mouth sunken with its weight. >

Beaty I don't want to hear this.

Alfa You can always tell who got rid of their baby.

Beaty (*overlapping*) Enough, that's enough.

Alfa In a room full of people, or walking down a crowded road, you can always tell . . .

Beaty I'm not listening.

Alfa (*continuing, oblivious*) It leaves its traces – an ugliness, a sorrow, a –

Beaty I've stopped listening to you. Oi! Deafie!

She sticks two fingers up at Alfa.

Coral (AD) < Beaty sticks two fingers up in a very un-Churchill-like kind of way. >

Beaty (*waving her fingers*) Sign language everyone can understand.

Alfa Only if you can see.

Beaty Just leave it – shut the fuck up, okay?

Alfa I hate being in the Chorus with you. You're an ugly person, Beaty, did you know that?

Beaty I'm ugly?

Alfa I'm not talking appearance; I'm talking inside. Ugly ugly ugly.

Beaty Watch it.

Alfa Ugly ugly ugly.

Beaty You're so ugly, your mother didn't give birth to you. She shat you.

Alfa You're so ugly, when you were born, the midwife slapped your mother.

Beaty I'm so ugly, I had the baby and she was taken away from me. Yeah . . . Because I'm what's ill-advisedly known as a 'handicap', a 'retard', a 'special person with special needs' and because I'm 'special', *apparently* I'm especially incapable of grasping the concept of contraception or looking after a baby. Or so the experts said. And because I'm a freaky damaged sick chick and because I have an interesting and increasingly rare genetic conjunction, it's best to tie the tubes – no, better still to slice them – as we don't want the special egg meeting with the sperm again, do we? We don't want any more special babies born because they're expensive, a drain on limited welfare resources and, let's face it, they don't really do much, do they? And while we're on the subject, let's be frank, 'normal' society finds 'special' scary and would much rather have them put down – did I say that, oops, I meant sterilise the fuckers, stop their depraved genes in their tracks, stop that freaky evolution, we don't like special, we want all to be the same and so during the caesarean when my apparently normal not-at-all-special baby was delivered, this special mum received a special operation, without consent or knowledge, to ensure no further specials were conceived. And it took me years to find out as they didn't think it important to inform me I was made sterile.

Coral But they can't do that!

Beaty No?

Long pause.

Coral I'm sorry.

Beaty Not as much as I am. (*aggressively, in the style of Chorus*) The last of my line.
A full stop.
The blank page following the final chapter in a book.

Coral And the baby?

Beat.

What happened to the baby? Did the baby survive?

Beaty Yes.

Coral Was the baby adopted? Beaty? Was the baby adop –?

Beaty – By a nice non-disabled family with a life expectancy much longer than the biological mother's. And that's all I'm gonna say about it.

Coral But –?

57

Beaty It's none of your fucking business.

Coral But we've just . . .

Beaty I work with you, you're not my best friend and just because we've both had a bun in the oven doesn't mean we're sisters under the skin.

Coral Beaty, you just told me . . .

Beaty (*interrupting*) We haven't shared anything significant, just an unfortunate coincidence . . .

Coral But the baby, the . . .

Beaty If you put a slice of brown bread with garlic and some parsley into the microwave for less than a minute, then eat it up quickly before it goes hard – you'll have a nice something for when you're in from work – feeling tired and wanting a snack. And the parsley's great as it gets rid of the garlic smell . . .

Coral Stop it! Just chitchat, chit-fucking-chit chat.

Beaty Don't you like chit-chat?

Coral No, I don't fucking like chit-chat and I don't like garlic on brown fucking sliced bread.

Beaty What about ciabatta? Seeded bread rolls, rye bread? How about thinly sliced white bleached processed bread . . . ?

Alfa (*to Beaty*) I like that German one. What is it? Pumpernickel?

Coral Don't you ever take anything seriously?

Beaty No. Because life's too short . . . or apparently in my case not as short as my mother or the medical profession led me to believe . . . I lost my little girl. Every day I think of her. Every day I think I could have been with her, whilst I'm living *now* and they said I'd be rotting in my grave. After that, I never want to take anything seriously again. So good old Coral . . . good on you, having a bun in the oven. A little loaf. Your yeasty high-riser. What kind is it, eh? Irish soda bread – was the daddy a paddy? Or petit pain – maybe he was French . . .

Coral Beaty . . .

Beaty Or a Scottish griddle cake . . .

Alfa (AD) < Beaty has gone off in a world of her own. >

Beaty Maybe Italian focaccia . . .

Alfa (AD) < Beaty lists all the bread she can remember. >

Beaty Well, there's always the American Wonder Loaf.

Alfa (AD) < As she does so, Alfa signs a story in BSL – the story she wants to tell – >

Beaty Sweet zucchini bread . . .

Alfa (AD) < – a terrible one, about warfare and eugenics . . . >

> *Alfa signs her story using* BSL, *but with no voice, whilst Beaty very slowly lists the breads. It may take some time, finishing just slightly before Alfa's signed story ends.*

Beaty Sourdough balls; baguette; walnut pavé; organic sundried tomato and basil plait; Hovis; Sunblest; Nimble; wholemeal bloomer; cholla; oaty tin; cheese and onion bread; panini; garlic and coriander naan; chapatis; pitta bread; poppyseed rolls; floury baps; warburtons; scofa; Irish boxty; pappadums; French stick; wheatgerm.

> *The following is a spoken English language précis of what Alfa will sign in performance, using* BSL *only and no voice. It is reproduced in this version solely for the purposes of the published text.*

Another version of this speech occurs in Scene Three, with a translation of BSL *into spoken English.*

Alfa (ALL IN BSL, ONLY. NO VOICE) A story starting a long time ago, in the war. A woman. Her community was uprooted and replanted in alien soil. She saw many things. The cruelty of men and women. A baby's nose gnawed away by a rat. Men and women starved so their ribs showed. This way the laboratories. This way the crematoriums. Many had not survived. She was taken the experimental route, along with the others – those who were blind, or had polio, and a plethora of other conditions and disabilities, including her own, which was to be deaf. She survived, along with others with an invisible sensory disability – who could almost 'pass'. She was useful. Could work. She was 'allowed' to survive – but with one amendment. They made her the last in her line – they sterilised all the men and women. After . . . she was repatriated to England – and lived in a small flat on the outskirts of London. She was grateful. She avoided her relatives. She found a companion, a quiet, troubled man who had been in a similar situation as she. They didn't speak of it. They didn't speak at all. They married. They had no children. People asked: why don't you have children? Why can't you have children? Are you sterile, then? Mule. Is that what you are, then, a sterile mule? They were silent. They did not speak about it. The war was over – ten, twenty, forty years and she was silent – he was silent – waiting for the knock on the door, the butt of a revolver against the skull, the bludgeoning hammer to fall. She lived daily with fear of violence should she tell what happened to her in the camps. She was one of hundreds, perhaps thousands . . . subjects of former experiments, trapped behind their net curtains, caught in a binding agreement not to tell never to tell. All stuck. All silent. Our story. (*with voice*) Schtump.

*Alfa's signing of the story and Beaty's naming of
bread come to an end. A pause.
    Coral looks at Alfa expectantly.*

Alfa (*with voice*) I'm not going to voice-over for you, so
don't look at me expecting an interpretation.

Coral But . . . I . . . but . . . but you . . .

Alfa It's not a secret language. It's in the public domain.

Coral But . . . I . . .

Alfa I'm not going to cheapen my exquisite signing with
your words.

Coral But you . . . but, but . . .

Alfa (*signed only*) JAWJAWJAWJAW, BLOODY TALKIES,
ALWAYS EATING AIR. (*with voice*) Learn it yourself.

*Several beats.
    The floods come on – Beaty moves downstage,
caught in a spotlight for the parallel play.*

Chorus

Beaty
    All men know children mean more than life.
    Which is why they kill them.

Blackout.

Three

*A huge wall of sound – loud music with explosions,
sirens and gunfire beneath.*

*When the lights come up, the women are out of their
silk dresses, wearing worn clothes. The sounds continue
intermittently throughout the start of the scene. The
women do not react to them, except as a brief silence,
then continuing with their speech/actions.*

*The women are involved in small, slowed activities.
Coral removing her costume, Beaty sewing a small white
(as yet unrecognisable) garment. Alfa is heating the soup
she was making earlier, with a travel electrical element.
Later, she passes around bowls and they eat. They speak
a 'non-chorus' at the opening: i.e., they are no longer the
Chorus, although they still assume the form. They speak in
their usual voices, everyday, tired, with no performance
mode. Even the audio description (AD) is closer to their
usual voices and lacks the presentation of before. There
are no floods.*

Non-chorus:

Alfa And as the trumpets

Beaty wailing

Coral all-clear sounded, the women came forward to
harvest their fallen fruit. Fields ripe with a strange crop

Alfa limbs

Beaty torsos

Alfa arms

Coral heads

All plucked

Coral ready to be gathered.

Beaty Here a hand relaxed, palm open, lying as it did so frequently in life.

Coral Here a body, soft, almost in repose

Beaty faces twisted

Coral teeth bared

Alfa eyes rolled back

All dead.

Coral All dead.

Alfa They claim them, the living, crawling across the rubble

Beaty seeking the familiar known faces

Alfa remembered hands

Coral half-forgotten birthmarks

Beaty flesh that when new was bathed, kissed, patted dry, powdered

Alfa sung over

Beaty lullabyed

Alfa Mamma's precious

Coral Future joy

Beaty now rank

Alfa sullied

Beaty gone forever.

All Child. Child.

   Beat.

Coral They've forgotten about us.

Beat.

Alfa (*to Coral*) Soup?

Coral (*to Alfa*) Yes, please.

Alfa (AD) < Alfa finds a soup bowl for Coral. > (*as self*) It's awfully quiet. Can you see the other side of the screen?

Beaty No.

Alfa I hate being behind a screen. I seem to spend my life behind a screen. I –

Coral Is anyone else feeling the heat? Have they switched off the air conditioning?

Alfa (*to Beaty*) Soup?

Beaty Yes.

Coral (AD) < Coral loosens her clothing. She sees everybody's face is beaded with sweat. >

Alfa (AD) < They eat. >

Several beats as they eat.

Coral Once. Once there was a Trojan horse wheeled in through the gates of the city, with death hidden in its belly. An intelligent betrayal. Violence contained. Death controlled. Now it just falls from the sky. It has no boundaries. It's invisible. War without frontiers. Or states. Or –

Alfa Has anybody got any painkillers?

Coral – identification. It's faceless.

Beaty I can do you codeine, Ibuprofen, Benylin, Night Nurse or Aspro.

Alfa Nothing stronger?

Beaty Quaaludes and cipro?

Coral We sit eating oven-ready dinners on our laps in front of the telly, the volume turned low, whilst food parcels are dropped in the middle of minefields.

Alfa I can't remember that speech from the play.

Coral The food we eat is poisoned. There are more wars raging now than in previous centuries put together.

Alfa Is she rehearsing a new scene?

Coral As the ice caps melt, the land will be submerged. The planet is dying. We inject it with cancers and yet we still procreate, we still continue the old dance, covering our eyes, feet stamping the rhythm, Mamma's precious, future joy.

Beaty I think her hormones are fucking her over. Gone tired and emotional, have we? A bit weepy?

Coral Fuck. You.

Beaty That oestrogen's a right bastard. Just chill. Have some more nice soup and borrow my mobile, call your boyfriend and give him the good news.

Coral Don't Patronise Me.

Beat.

Alfa It's really quiet.(AD) < Alfa stares out into the darkness before her. > Why can't we see out? Have they brought the fire curtain down? Has everybody been sent home? It really has gone awfully quiet.

Beaty And you'd be able to tell the difference?

Coral Don't start.

Alfa Is it over?

Beat.

Did anyone hear the applause?

Beat.

Was everyone sent home?

Beat.

Didn't the audience come back after the third interval?

Coral It's an epic, all right.

Alfa I've no idea what act I'm in. Where am I? Where was I?

Coral Women. Children. Variations on a theme.

Beaty Men.

Coral Yeah, men. Women. Children. War. Women being strong.

Beaty Killing their babies. (AD) < Alfa flinches. >

Alfa I don't think I like this play very much.

Beaty So when did you have your abortion?

A shocked silence.

Coral (AD) < Alfa closes her eyes, cutting out all communication. >

Alfa speaks/signs the following at breakneck speed, without punctuation.

Alfa It was supposed to be the ideal perfect punctuation two people who love each other plus baby full stop baby made up from each other as though we could disassemble ourselves then reinvent two as three and it was perfect right from the start we felt we were doing more than making love we really were making life and I knew even

66

before the pregnancy test I could feel it like there was a fizzing in my blood a secret I shared with my tissues and bones the fleshy matter that made up me and the father moved in and we booked the registry office and I (*slower*) arranged for an amniocentesis test . . .

Coral (AD/*storyteller*) < Alfa opens her eyes. She shrugs, drops her eloquent hands. They lie in her lap, palms up, as though unable – or unwilling – to shape the words to come. >

Alfa What destroyed us was trying to decide where to put the blame. These two making three . . . when the sums don't add up – when the calculations are faulty – when the perfect multiplication comes out wrong – who made the mistake? Whose was the rogue gene? Who brought the unwanted guest to the intimate family dinner? We discovered a hierarchy of acceptability. He didn't mind a sensory disability; he didn't mind me being Deaf.

Beaty That's really big of him.

Coral Ssssh.

Alfa But when it came to that missing chromosome . . . I know what I'm supposed to think, I know what's right-on, I know what I'm *supposed* to *do*, but . . . I couldn't do it. The effort – the work involved – the never-ending dedication that was required, having a rewarding but exhausting child, for ever and ever – I couldn't do it. Okay? I couldn't fucking do it. And then I realised nobody needed to know. I could keep my political correctness and my disability awareness and my halo still shining. I could remain holier than thou and get rid of it, flush it away, throw the blood-clot in the bin. So I did. And I asked the father to return my keys, pack his toothbrush and go off and worship some other flawed goddess, because I didn't deserve love, I needed to be

67

punished. And I'm still serving time. So do you have a problem with that?

Beaty (AD) < She looks at me, then out towards the auditorium. >

Alfa Have they forgotten about us? Have they all gone home?

Beaty (AD) < Beaty takes Alfa's bag of knittiing and empties it of finished garments. She begins laying the clothing on the floor, adding her own contribution: tiny white matinee jackets; a new-born baby's vest; booties . . . >

She does so, covering the floor with the baby clothing, including the white garment she has been sewing – a baby's vest. Alfa joins her. They continue the action through the following.
A shift again in style and place.
When they make a statement about war, the women speak slowly with dignity, low-key.

Beaty They rounded up all the men and male children and brought them to the stadium. The grass now grows over them.

Coral They bombed the people in the bread queue, then shot those trying to comfort the dying.

Beaty They killed all the boys a moment before their fathers, so the men could see their hopes destroyed.

Coral Yesterday, four pupils were killed at their desks at school.

Beaty There was an explosion in the market place. People lay scattered. Blood flowered on a woman's face.

Alfa repeats a version of the BSL *eugenics speech of Scene Two, this time without sign language, but vocalising* BSL. *Instructions in italics are placement.*

Alfa Happen war past.   People force move strange place.   Woman there watch watch.   See bad things like what? Baby rat crawl up baby gnaw. People cruel. Men women food nothing   go thin   ribs. Strange place have what? (*Points left.*) Science test. (*Points right.*) House fire bury   people pile in   burnt. Woman in where? (*Points left.*) Science test. Many people them have what? Disability blind weak the shakes the limp. Some see, some hidden.   Woman (*Points index.*) she what? Deaf. She get away. Many people die. Bith finish. She not. She useful. Work. She live-win can. Allowed. But (*Points left.*) happen what? Men penis cut. Woman insert cut. Birth children stop. Finish. Many many die. Many live-win not. She live-win. War finish   woman go where? England. Live London outside. She relief-thankful.   Woman meet meet family? No. Woman. (*Points right.*) Man. (*Points left.*) Meet partner   marry join. Children have p-hho. People ask p-hho children why? Problem what? Insert cut bin both? You yaah damage? You yaah destroy? Sterile you? Stomach suck out bin? She tell past no. He tell past no. Couple schtum always   discuss nothing   schtump. Life progress, ten, twenty, forty years progress. She continue silent. Why? Continue wait for what?   Soldier   guns   door   bash bash bam beat.   Bin told before, 'You let know bin insert cut   we you punish suffer suffer more hup.' She every day continue   live how? Schtump. Why? If tell, punish. Frighten frighten. Life danger. She alone no. Many many same. All over house house house house people people people people   stuck stuck stuck stuck. Fix forget never say nothing fear inside body schtump want release mouth not allowed zip mouth. Our story schtump. All schtump

Pause.

Beaty Have the baby.

69

A change back.

Have the bloody baby.

Beat.

To make up for those we've lost.

Alfa (AD) < We glance sideways at each other, eyes swivelling, avoiding direct contact. >

Coral Oh yeah, right – let's all go out and have babies as some response to the holocaust. Or if not that atrocity, some other war; there's plenty to choose from. And if the baby isn't disabled, what do we do then? Get rid of it?

Alfa (AD) < Temperature rising – a rush of blood to my face. >

Coral 'Cause we want the 'whacky' genes, the 'impairments', right?

Alfa (AD) < A nervous tic beneath my right eye – morse code tapping out all is not well. >

Coral Let's go procreate to ensure in the future there's still an excluded underclass. Let's fill the day centres and institutions with another generation undervalued by the rest of the country. Let's have children so they'll suffer the pain we can hardly bear; let them continue with the same struggle for basic human rights; the numbing round of political and social campaign. Sure, let's patent our genes so no multinational pharmaceutical company can wipe us out, as we have such high quality of life we want more to experience it.

Beaty You talk such bullshit.

Coral No. I know what I'm *supposed* to think – what is right-on to say – but this isn't a political theory, this is my life and I'm not convinced I want another poor bastard to go through everything I have.

Several beats. The women reflect. They go into performance Chorus-mode – no floods – this is their own version.

They begin to remove and discard the remains of their costumes.

Alfa
So they made a decision, those women with their phantom children.

Beaty
These women who knew in which direction the world revolved: counter to them.

Alfa
They smelt the ash of a thousand burning bodies, watching the bruise deepen on the delicate flesh where the earth and the sky met.

Coral
And these women knew the stories and they knew what would happen.

Alfa
So they taught their children to dance.

Beaty
Mamma's precious

Coral
Future joy.

Alfa
They taught their children to dance and, clasping hands, they danced up along the city gates

Beaty
as the bruise deepened on the horizon,

Alfa
they danced out, along the city's upper walls, past the lookout,

Beaty
mother's faces wet with tears

Alfa
beyond the cobbled roads, where the path stumbled into rock and mud they danced, up along the steep incline –

Beaty
– hands clasped, tiny feet stamping the rhythm.

Alfa
Mamma's precious

Coral
Future joy.

They stop. A beat.

Alfa (*to Coral*) Did you know you can make oranges less messy to eat by putting them in the freezer for half an hour before peeling them?

Coral Just fucking get on with it . . .

Alfa With . . .?

A pause.

Beaty (AD) < They are silent. They do not move. >

Beat.

Coral I think I'm bleeding.

Immediate blackout.

End.